The Prophecies of Paracelsus

Paracelsus

© 2023 Culturea Editions
Texte et illustration de couverture : © domaine public
Edition : Culturea (Hérault, 34)
Contact : infos@culturea.fr
Retrouvez notre catalogue sur http://culturea.fr
Imprimé en Allemagne par Books on Demand
Design typographique : Derek Murphy
Layout : Reedsy (https://reedsy.com/)
ISBN : 9791041943012
Dépôt légal : janvier 2023
Tous droits réservés pour tous pays

Contents

Proem

THE Prophecies of Paracelsus attracted my attention at an early stage of my studies in the Occult, which have now extended to over forty years, but I have only recently thought of bringing them to public notice, the extraordinary events of the present time acting as an incentive.

The famous French Kabbalist, Alphonse Louis Constant, in *La Clef des Grands Mystères*, p. 378, wrote:

'The Prophecy of Paracelsus, of which we here give the Preface, is composed of thirty-two chapters with allegorical figures.

'It is the most astounding monument and indisputable proof of the reality and existence of the gift of natural prophecy.'

Abbé Constant (born 1809, died 1875), better known by his Hebraistic pseudonym, Eliphas Lévi Fahed, was a distinguished Adept, Magus, and Writer on the Occult. Most of his works have been ably translated by Mr. A. E. Waite.

The Preface Eliphas Lévi refers to is not given here, but will be found preceding the Predictions.

The Prophecies of Paracelsus

Eliphas Lévi then continues:

'Following this Preface commence a series of figures.

'The first represents two millstones, the two powers of the state, the people and the aristocracy; but the people's stone is crossed by a serpent holding a bundle of birchrods in its jaws; a hand armed with a sword comes out of a cloud and seems to direct the serpent, which overthrows the millstone and causes it to fall upon the other.

'The second figure represents a dead tree, the fruits of which are *fleur-de-lys*, and the text announces the exile of the family of whom the *fleur-de-lys* is the emblem.

'Farther on the millstone, representing the people, falls upon a crown and breaks it.

'Farther on still a bishop is shown immersed in water and surrounded by spears that prevent him from reaching the bank. In the text it says:

'"Thou hast come out of thy bounds, now thou demandest the earth, but it will not be surrendered to thee."

(The German text is slightly different.)

'Then can be seen an eagle hovering over the Bosphorus, where the Sultan appears to be drowning.)

And as this eagle has not two heads and is not black Eliphas Lévi considers that this excludes Russia and Austria.

The great French Kabbalist then concludes:

'*It would perhaps not be prudent at present to publish the remainder.* Curious persons can consult the Latin book printed with the title *Prognosticatio eximii doctoris Theophrasti Paracelsi*, which should be found in the National Libraries.

'We possess two copies, one in manuscript and the other photographed after a copy printed in the sixteenth century.'

Thus far Eliphas Lévi in 1861; this is the year 1915.

Now the world is in the throes of a great European war, there is no reason why these pregnant Prophecies should any more be kept secret, and every reason why they should be widely known.

Great changes in the world are before us, both in Religion and Politics. Considering the importance at the present critical time of a clearer outlook, this glimpse into the future coming from the past may not be inopportune, and the present publication of the Predictions of Paracelsus may assist and interest, both from a religious and political point of view, all who are concerned in the world's progress. It may also serve to aid the reader to a better acquaintance with the great Adept of the Renaissance, when his own quaint words on Past, Present, and Future are reproduced.

INTRODUCTORY   1.   CONCERNING PARACELSUS

THEOPHRASTUS BAUMBAST VON HOHENHEIM, commonly known as Paracelsus, the famous Swiss Physician, Alchemist and Occultist of the sixteenth century, was born on the 10th November, 149 3, at Sihlbrücke, near Einsiedeln, Canton Schwyz, and died on the 24th September, 1541, at Salzburg.

Contemporary with Charles V, Luther, Erasmus, and Cornelius Agrippa, Paracelsus stands out as an extraordinary character that has been for a long time misunderstood by the majority of the learned and unlearned alike.

Living in the age of the Reformation, siding neither with Catholic nor Protestant, he distinguished himself as a free lance in Medical Science and Occult Philosophy, and would have been known as a Mystic had his religious writings not been so carefully suppressed as to be altogether forgotten. Paracelsus then claims our attention as Alchemist, Physician, Occultist, Mystic, Astrologer and lastly as Prophet, and it is in this last capacity that we shall regard him, as we are about to study and thereby rescue from oblivion those at one time famous predictions, of which some have been remarkably accomplished,, while others may be considered to be still in actual course of fulfilment.

Concerning the life of this remarkable man we are informed that his first teacher was his father, the learned Wilhelm Baumbast von Hohenheim, a physician, who took pains to instruct him in all the learning of the time, especially in Medicine.

At the age of sixteen young Baumbast entered the University of Basle. But he soon abandoned academic studies, preferring the mystic and occult teachings of the famous Adept, Johannes Trithemius, Abbot of Spanheim, a noted Alchemist and Divine, whose ideas he absorbed.

However, he soon forsook the Abbot, as he had previously forsaken University culture, to study Metallurgic Chemistry in the mines then owned by the Fuggers in Tyrol.

It is not my intention to give a description of the Life of Paracelsus, as such an excellent account appears of him in the eleventh edition of the *Encyclopaedia Britannica.*

Fuller biographical details are given in *The Life of Paracelsus*, by Dr. Edward Berdoe, M.R.C.S., in the Life and Teachings of Paracelsus, by Franz Hartmann, M.D., and in *The Life of Paracelsus* by Anne M. Stoddart.

Those who read German will find interesting details in the little volume, *Theophrastus Paracelsus, sein Leben und seine Persönlichkeit,* by Franz Strunz.

I must, however, differ from the last-named author, who would claim Paracelsus for the Pantheon of German fame and would endeavour to prove that he was a German. He was not. Paracelsus, although he preferred to lecture and write in German, was all his life, heart, soul and backbone, a Swiss. This *en passant.*

Paracelsus, in his book Von der grossen Wundarznei, volunteers concerning himself the following information: 'From childhood upward have I followed these studies and received instruction from those experienced in Adept Philosophy.'

He then mentions his principal teachers. 'First, Wilhelm von Hohenheim, my father, who never failed me.

'I studied the writings of ancients and moderns, and had a number of teachers I can hardly name.

'Some of them took great trouble with me, such as the Bishops of Stettgach, of Lavantall, and of Yppen, the Abbot of Spanheim, and further, Sigmund Fugger von Schwatz, and many workers in his laboratory.'

Fugger may have largely influenced his mind in Alchemy, but in the recently unearthed theological writings of Paracelsus mentioned by Professor Karl Sudhoff in his learned work *Versuch einer Kritik der Echtheit der Paracelsischen Schriften*, 2. vols., Berlin, 1894-1899, we find a clear indication that he derived his prophetic gift from that source of all Prophecy--Mystic Illumination.

Paracelsus--he assumed that name when he began to teach, to indicate his superiority to Celsus--was for all his numerous instructors, to a great extent, like all adepts, self-taught and soul-inspired.

A mystic leading a sexless life, he had glimpses of Cosmic Consciousness or Divine Illumination, far transcending the knowledge of his time, and while under such inspiration, that secret spring of all genius and prophecy, he wrote and said more than he knew in his mortal mind.

Searching for knowledge and truth, roving through various countries, practising and teaching a system of empirical medicine which we will not here discuss, he got into touch with life in all its phases, and into a state of mind most favourable to the attainment of that Kabbalistic state of Cosmic Consciousness, or Divine Illumination, which rays forth throughout his luminous writings.

Famous, yet hated and persecuted by unprogressive contemporaries, misunderstood by the unenlightened of the following centuries, posterity has at last vindicated the fame and character of this hero of Occult Science.

Professor Strunz observes of Paracelsus:

'His was a mind of mighty features whose rare maturity converted the stating of scientific problems into warm human terms, and we owe to him the realisation of a cultured human community based upon Christian and humanitarian piety and faith, which things we may well regard as the bases of his teaching concerning both the actual and the spiritual. His restless life never robbed him of that witchery which ever and again flushed the immortal impulses of his soul like golden sunshine; that vision which belongs to the great nature-poet. And yet few men of his time recognised, as he did, the incalculable result to be attained by the empiric-inductive method. . . . Paracelsus felt like an artist and thought like a mathematician, just as he combined the laws of nature with the laws of the microcosm, that is of man with his consciousness, his feelings, and his desires. It was this delicate artistic sense which proved to be the daring bridge from the man Paracelsus to the keen-visioned observer of reality, a wondrous viaduct resting upon the traverses of the new humanity, the Renascence. For upon this viaduct moved forward that reconstruction of the universe of which Paracelsus was one of the greatest architects.'[1]

The poet Robert Browning made Paracelsus the subject of one of his finest poems, describing him as an idealist and student of Nature's mysteries.

Professor Dowden in his Biography 'Robert Browning' explains the poem 'Paracelsus' as follows:

'The poem is the history of a great spirit, who has sought lofty and unattainable ends, who has fallen upon the way and is bruised and broken, but who rises at the close above his ruined self and wrings out of defeat a pledge of ultimate victory.

'Paracelsus as presented in the poem is a man of pre-eminent genius, passionate intellect, and inordinate intellectual ambition. If it is meant that he should be the type of the modern man -of science Browning has missed his mark, for Paracelsus is in fact as much the poet as the man of science . . .

'Paracelsus is a great revolutionary spirit in an epoch of intellectual revolution; it is as much his task to destroy as to build up; he has broken with the past, and gazes with wild-eyed hopes into the future, expecting the era of intellectual liberty to dawn suddenly with the year One, and seeing himself the protagonist of Revolution.

'Such men as Paracelsus, whether their sphere be in the political, the religious, or the intellectual world, are men of faith; a task has been laid on each of them; a summons, a divine mandate, has been heard. But is the mandate indeed divine?

'Very nobly has Browning represented the overmastering force of that faith, which genius has in itself, and which indeed is needed in the struggle with an incredulous or indifferent world!

Introductory 2. On The Prophecies Of Paracelsus

'THE world, as the Eddas say, is ruled by three Fates, the Past, the Present, and the Future. The Present rests upon the Past and proceeds from it, the Future from the Present. But it is the Future that holds the ideal to which the world moves, and therefore it is she who conditions both the Present and the Past. The Three are inextricably One.'--H. Fielding Hall, *The World Soul.*

THERE is not the slightest doubt that if the Present is the result of the Past, the Future will be the result of the Present. The three being one, the Future should be as easily read as the Past. But this can only be done when the finite mind of the Seer becomes one with the infinite mind of the Seen, by a manifestation of the Soul, which is the Creator, and source of Truth.

The Prophecies of Paracelsus are set forth in thirty-two 'magical' or allegorical Figures with Prognostications to each Figure, a Preface and an Epilogue or Elucidation written by Paracelsus.

The entire work evidently relates to predictions of mundane events, some to ecclesiastical affairs, others to social political upheavals and changes that have since happened, are actually becoming accomplished or may still come to pass.

The Predictions, apparently limited to 24 or 42 years (both numbers are given) from 1530, about which time they appeared, were possibly occultly intended to mean mystic years, meaning either the fulness of time, or 240 or 420 years, which latter term would include the affairs of the present critical time.

Whoever studies these predictions cannot fail to see how worldly affairs have followed the course Paracelsus foretold for them either by mystic inspiration or astrological calculation.

Concerning the time when certain predictions should come to pass, an eminent seer of the Middle Ages, the Hermit Johannes Liechtenberger, aptly observed:

'Although Almighty God alone has retained the time and hour in his power, and he alone knows future things, and although there is no one in this world who can predict anything with certainty for to-morrow, or for some days to come, nevertheless the same merciful Deity, of his overflowing Love, has poured various gifts unto his creatures, whereby in things that are still distant and in the future, He allows us to understand and know, not wholly, but in divers parables, symbols and comparisons of things already happened with those that are to take place in the future.'

These Predictions were at their first publication in great demand and often reprinted.

Professor Sudhoff mentions numerous editions and reprints, but they would have fallen altogether into oblivion had not the noted Kabbalist, Eliphas Lévi, drawn attention to them by counselling their suppression.

True Initiates are ever on the side of Law and Order, and maintain that the secrets of the Occult should remain occult. But these are times when the old order changes and what has been kept occult must become manifested.

The time has thus arrived for making known what has been kept in concealment or lapsed into oblivion for centuries; for as Paracelsus quaintly observes: 'when the time comes then comes also that wherefore the time has come.'

In that extremely rare, because suppressed, occult book, *A Suggestive Inquiry into the Hermetic Mystery*, occurs the remarkable observation:

'Many prophecies there are of times to come, and those days are even said to be at hand, when the Fourth Monarchy, which is the Intellectual reign of Truth and Peace, shall predominate, when the Mother of Sciences will come forth, and greater things be discovered than have been hitherto in the past monarchies of the world. But we do not tarry about these matters; the Revelation of all things is always at hand for him who knows how to investigate, and the rest will be always far behind. If truly there be minds prepared, or if the great era approaches more rapidly than is given us yet even in faith to foresee (for notwithstanding so many signs that are appearing, all signal rumours of a coming change, yet they are fewer and far between and more rare yearly which indicate the progression of Truth); but if, we say, a better age is approaching, which at some period of time must come, when abundance of all things by an equitable distribution of all, shall help to break down the competitive barrier of society, and introduce a co-operative alliance among mankind, then this incentive to inquiry may not be inopportunely offered in the self-discovery of truth.'

Curiously enough Paracelsus also connects the establishment of the 'Fourth Monarchy' or Millennium with a rediscovery of Alchemy and a universal knowledge of the secret of transmutation of metals.

'Then will the Old Art flourish, and no heed be given to the New.

'Then shall the Pearl so long lost be found by an humble one, and will be set, as a jewel, in gold,' etc.

What the world would be if gold had to be demonetised on account of its being as common as lead I must leave to the reader's imagination.

The idea of the Millennium may also have served as an occult allegory for the Regeneration of Man, as every reborn Soul lives even now in the Millennium, the Fourth or Fifth Monarchy, or the Rule of Christ.

The attainment of the Individual to the Divine mystic state of Illumination would in no wise impede, but rather hasten, the realisation of the Father's Kingdom on earth.

Paracelsus calls the Power that rules the world's Fate, Magic.

The Creator rules the world by Magic. He is the Divine Magician creating and sustaining the All by His omnipotent *Word*: Fiat! Be!

Man, too, has the Soul-Power of Magic, but it extends no further than the potency of his trained will and the reality of his Thought.

The Creator's Will being omnipotent, Man's will is only potent in as far as it is in unison with the Creator's.

But Man by selfishness circumscribes his power and dissevers himself from the Eternal Unself, the I AM.

Were Man to enter the plane of the Divine Unself his power for Good would increase in proportion to his attunement with the Father's Will.

But clouded by ignorance and environed by sin, that has become his lower Nature, man's mind knows nothing of the Reality of the Eternal Mind nor of its Mastery over Fate.

Man, as he now is, has depraved senses but no real Thought. He is but the creature of a day, and perishes like the beasts he devours, having fallen from Providence to Fate.

Who can tell the extent of the faculties Man possesses when he is in his rightful state--the Immortal Mind?

Who can even faintly foreshadow the vast power latent in his eternal Being?

Can the son of the Infinite be finite?

Is it not more probable that he too has faculties for infinite development?

Why should the Future not be known to us as the Past?

The Soul knows all things, the Soul being the Eternal Mind.

The self-inflicted eclipse of the Soul will not last for ever.

Sin is the result of Ignorance and Ignorance the cause of sin.

Where true knowledge flourishes sin dies and man becomes a regenerate being.

Let us therefore endeavour to understand the everpresence of the Creator in the World and in Nature.

Wherever we rightly search Nature's phenomena we can infer from Manifestation to Cause, from Cause to Thought, from Thought to Law, from Law to Love.

Nature, when rightly understood, will be seen to act upon the principles of Thought that we can follow, of Love that we can love and that loves us.

By Nature we mean the creative Life in Nature.

Man should not be subject to Fate, as he now is, but should be a Divine being guarded by Providence, the Divine Mind.

If we could only realise that we are immortal beings, how differently we should live!

Let us then, endeavour to understand the everpresence of the Creator in Nature.

Underlying Phenomena there are Noumena, underlying Nature there is Nature's God--the Creator. Sustaining Matter there is the all-pervading Spirit.

The Universe is not void, the Universe is full. Ether holds all things in solution.

Wherever we can follow the Creator's footsteps in Nature or in History, we find revelations of Divine Thought.

Nature's Law is animated by Divine Thought.

He, the Creator, is united to us as the Spirit of Life, the All Soul, the All Life. Our Soul, our Life is a part of His.

We are the Creator's offspring, but we can only become children of the Father's Kingdom by an act of mystic self-renunciation. The renunciation of Self--the lower Nature.

We may now inquire *how* these predictions were given by Paracelsus.

Although predictions can be made by the aid of Astrology alone and their subsequent accomplishment may be deemed marvellous, yet no one will have a correct foresight unless he sees with the eye of the Soul, whereby comes a true image of things seen in the Eternal Mind.

Concerning this true Imagination Paracelsus says in his *Liber de Imaginibus*, Cap. XII:

'Therefore should you also know that the perfect Imagination coming from the Astral, issues from the Soul, wherein all Astra lie occult, and the Soul, Faith and Imagination, are three things to count, for the names are different, but they have equal force and strength, for one comes from the other, and I cannot compare it otherwise than with the Divine Trinity. For through the Soul we come to God, through Faith to Christ and through the Imagination to the Divine Spirit. Therefore also is to these three, even as to the Divine Trinity, nothing impossible.'

In the time of Paracelsus it was not safe to know anything beyond the dogmas of Mother Church. We find therefore that most real knowledge became occult.

The Prognostications were given in signs and symbols and to interpret them we will let Paracelsus himself give us a few hints.

In the same Book, Cap. V, he explains.:

'When out of *Magic* a Prophecy is given by pictures and figures, on a city, country, government, principality or kingdom, it is indicated by the animals, arms, colours which the same city, country, prince, or king carries, and not described in plain words.

'Therefore every one who would undertake to interpret such Prophecy, should not only be a good Astrologer but also a good Magnus and should know thoroughly what plant, animal or colour each city, country, prince or Lord carries in the coat of arms.

'As an example, the Eagle means in Magic the Emperor, or only his Empire.

'Three Lilies, or only one Lily, the King of France, or the Kingdom of France.

'Three Crowns, one upon the other, or a triple cross, the Pope, or the entire Papacy.

'A crown by itself, a King or a Kingdom.

'A Half-Moon, the Sultan, or his Empire, and so on.'

France, the Papacy, the German Empire, England, Russia, Turkey, &c., appear in the Predictions many of which have been remarkably fulfilled.

The 'Magic' Paracelsus speaks of is the occult Divine Power that rules the Destiny of the World and the Regeneration of the

Individual Soul. It is the World Soul. I should prefer to call it the Creator's Everpresence.

According to the Kabbala every Nation has a Ruling Angel, Prince or Lord.

It is however also esoterically taught that the Archangels are not persons but dignities or grades which the Soul must attain before becoming united with the Creator.

Thus might the whole set of Figures and Texts be esoterically interpreted as the phases of the Soul's course towards Perfection, and what exoterically treats of the world's course or destiny may esoterically teach the Regeneration of the Soul.

This interpretation could be taken for each and all of the thirty-two figures and chapters.

It was a common practice for mediaeval Occultists to write about one subject, teaching all the while another.

Such policy was, in those times, necessary.

Even as a treatise on the Occult may these Prognostics be found of interest to those who are mystically inclined.

The XXXIInd Chapter is profoundly mystical. 'Blessed is he that is born during sleep' refers to the Divine re-birth, the birth of Cosmic Consciousness.

Thus, although the chapters and figures openly refer to the world, secretly they may speak of the world in Man.

Manifestly the Regeneration of the World is treated, occultly the Divine Re-birth in Man may be intended.

The Power at work in the one as in the other is that Mystic 'Magic,' the Divine Christ-Spirit.

According to Hebrew Tradition, the Incarnations of the Messiah educate mankind for perfection, while Christian Mystics maintain that the world is under the guardianship of Christ.

In the Occult Art of Regeneration it is the same Divine Spirit that teaches and guides the Soul in her course towards the 'End'--'Nirvana' the Divine Re-birth.

It is a peculiarity of true occult books that they bear looking into beneath the surface meaning, and the more their occult meaning is studied the more it will become manifest.

The Smaragdine Tablet of 'Hermes', *the Twelve Keys* of 'Basil Valentine' and the *Amphitheatrum* of Khunrath are considered to teach simultaneously Alchemy, 'Magic,' and the Kabbala.

These three are said to be not three Arts, but one Art relating to the body, spirit and soul of our being.

J.K.

Introductory 3. Eliphas Lévi's Preface To The Prognostications

IN *La Clef des Grands Mystères*, mentioned in the Prefatory Remarks, Eliphas Lévi gives: *The Preface to the Prognostication of Doctor Theophrastus Paracelsus*, of which the following is a translation:

'Socrates, discoursing one day upon the too curious research of celestial things, during which one forgets the realities of human life, and of the earth that lies at our feet, exclaims: "That which is above our comprehension does not exist for us"; wishing thereby to say that a timorous and superstitious consideration of the heavens is vain, useless and dangerous.

'It may be indeed that a wise man warned by his reason of peril may be deterred from such study. Elsewhere Socrates, in the Dialogues of Plato, everywhere praises moderation and balance in all things. It is thus that the words of this great philosopher should be understood; for there is no reason to suppose that he would calumniate astrology, he being himself, according to the testimony of Plato, an excellent Astrologer.

'I will not here essay an apology for a science honoured by many learned men, I will only say one word: that there is not another art that can so justly be called divine in its source, in its tradition and in its theory. Read Moses, he will tell you why God has placed in the firmament the sun, the moon, and the stars to be for signs and for seasons, and for days and for years; which inspires Saint Paul to praise those wise men of the world who have found and known in visible things their invisible Creator. It is true that he continues to blame them for not having honoured him more than the creature.

God wills, in fact, that we should be attentive to the law of the elements, in order to elevate ourselves from the work to its Author, to know and adore Him; for all appearances and all material forms are but marks and veils that allow the most intimate secrets of nature to be divined beneath them.

'Thus were those magnificent sciences invented, thus were those marvellous arts born, that make us discover in roots, in stones, and even in men powers occult to the vulgar and revealed only to the sagacity of those sages named by Hesiod and by Homer μεροπες, meropes, that is to say, great seekers.

'All the while let us not attribute too much to human intelligence. It is a divine Wisdom descending from the Father of Light, according to the text of St. James. God has given us characters forming letters; He has attached to them all the feelings of the Soul. Through them we can speak; through them as through a divine instrument, He transmits to us and teaches us every day the secrets of all sciences.

'God having thus adapted the wonders of creation to the use of man, has established from the beginning a school of initiation for that. Wisdom which all may not comprehend. There we learn with care the things hidden from the multitude. Thus the fisherman draws his net from the depths of the sea filled with fish that he never saw; the miners bring forth masses of gold and silver from the depths of the earth where the eye cannot penetrate. In this wise in the school of Nature God teaches us and places before our eyes things altogether unknown. Thus there is nothing hidden which shall not become revealed and placed in the light; be it in the firmament of the heavens, be it in the sea, be it in the earth, all must be brought forth to the light of the day by those great seekers of whom I have spoken.

'Meanwhile these celebrated men by their science cause their immortal names to pass from mouth to mouth; for they have in a manner cleared up Nature, and their memory should never become extinct. The muse never cedes her inheritance of glory to death. It is by genius that we live, all the rest belongs to death.

'In same wise, according to our powers and the gift of Providence, have we desired to glean after those noble harvesters and explained to the world the threatenings of Nature and of the stars, for a period to come, which is to last forty (query 400) years, in order that men may find themselves informed, learning to fear God, and to prepare themselves for the future chastisement of great crimes. It is impossible to express up to what point all flesh has corrupted its way. Anarchy is everywhere. Heaven and Earth are confounded, and were God not to shorten the days of His wrath no flesh could be saved. The disorderly life of men of my time is that which specially determined me carefully to study the stars.

'Now there are signs in the sun, the moon and the stars that announce the speedy coming of the judgment of God. The axe is at the foot of the tree, blood flows upon blood, and as the Prophet says, no one among men disturbs himself about God, there is not one who seeks Him. But the Prophets and Evangelists have at present the mission to recall us to charity, concord and unity. Unity is in the Divine Triad, and the Divine Triad is summarised in Unity.

'It is in this wise that in human society, unity, peace, and tranquillity should arise. When unity is broken, plurality of power immediately engenders discord and war. There are as many opinions as there are heads; each one would make his own triumphant; then there is no more harmony possible, but in unity there is rest with abundance of peace. O how well and pleasant it is for brothers to dwell in unity!

exclaims the prophet David. Unity is the happiness of all creatures. The Heavens have but one law of motion and harmony; the earth has but one law to produce love, and gives her fruit in season. All obey unity, except Satan and Man. Man, however, is sufficiently warned by the signs of heaven, by the sun, the moon and the stars . . . But what do these announce? He is too menaced with a sudden and quickly approaching end. Happy is he that sitteth not in the chair of pestilence, and walketh not in the counsel of scorners! The coming of God is at hand. The arm of the avenger falls on us; everyone feels the misfortunes coming which he cannot avoid.

'Who will then struggle against God? One kicks not against the pricks with impunity. The God of Hosts is the strong God, the jealous God, who visits the iniquities of the fathers upon the children to the fourth and fifth generation.

'Oppose God, what folly! Foolhardy Titans who would dethrone Jupiter were themselves overthrown by his thunder. It is time to show men their madness, and it is this we propose to do by thirty-two figures intelligible but to a small number of the elect.

'We have seen the consummate iniquity of the people of Gomorha, carrying their blasphemies unto the heavens; but when things are pushed to extremes, the overbent bow breaks, and men are driven by a fatal law to a contrary extremity, whereby motion relaxes and the balance is established.

'Thus by perpetrating crime after crime corruption shall exhaust itself; and who can sadden thereat? Behold the salvation of the multitude is coming and redemption shall overcome the kingdom of evil.

'Who would not be impatient to see the days where unity shall be given unto us and we shall live in peace under only one shepherd!

'Then no more troubles, no more injustice, the balm shall descend upon the venerable beard of the High-Priest, the blessing, light, gratitude to Heaven shall spread upon the children of unity.

'Pride having made itself odious even in Heaven, the faithful angels did not weep at the fall of Lucifer, they affirmed the Divine sentence.

'Let us therefore not grieve if God opens now His Hell under the feet of the haughty.

'Let us rather rejoice, for the judgment has commenced in the House of God itself, and it will thence extend upon every kind of unjust pride.

'Our prediction has hardly any other aim than to reveal, as we have said, the threatenings of Heaven against insolent heads.

'God desires to deliver and avenge finally His oppressed children Himself, He wishes to cast down the powerful and to lift up the humble. . . . But it is not yet there that the pains begin. The greatness of evil has not yet revealed itself; it shall reveal itself, and with it a force shall become manifested that will prevent the just from being seduced and drawn into the ruin of the perverse.

'We say that no one shall be named in our prophecy. God knows those whom He has resolved to chastise, men do not know Him, but they shall sooner feel that justice has overtaken them than we with our human sagacity can seek and divine. All is concealed and nevertheless revealed to us.

'The Kabbala always veiled, never pronounces oracles without mysteries, and we are assured that it is of her we receive Astrology. God blinds the eyes and hardens the heart of those whom He has delivered to His vengeance, for He no longer wishes to save them.

'In concluding this Preface I pray all those who will read these articles to interpret my words in simplicity and not to seek personalities under my emblems.

'Let them keep their minds free from all thoughts of hate, fear or envy. The event will strike in justice and then those who will shall know.

'I know many others have worked in the same direction, I do not despise either their knowledge nor their efforts, on the contrary I encourage them.

'I see death flying over many monastic institutions, but if men would be wise and were to return to God, He is merciful and good and allows Himself to be moved by the importunity of prayers.

'We do not attribute to the stars a fatal power, they impel us by their influence, but if the Master wills it, He alone can alter the direction and change all. Joshua prayed and the sun stood still to allow him to accomplish his victory. Hezekiah prayed and the shadow tarried on the sundial. Elijah prayed and the heavens closed. The continual prayer of the righteous is all powerful. Those who would avert the threatened danger have but to repent, to pray, to live wisely and soberly. God our Father gives us His Grace by Christ and in His Holy Spirit. Amen.'

This Preface is imbued with the Spirit of Paracelsus but differs from the Preface in the German edition of the Prognostications given in the following section.

Introductory 4. Strassburg Edition Of The Preface To The Prognostications

THIS Preface to the Prognostications was given in the Strassburg Edition of the Collected Works of Paracelsus, vol. ii, p. 594. It runs as follows:

'It may be questioned whether we can at all describe the effects of the stars, since we do not see that which passes even upon earth and what lies at our feet, and often stumble and strike against it; far less can we know of the Heavens. But the reply thereto is, that for this purpose we do not use our eyes nor our feet.

'Further can this instruction be given: it is God's will that we should have our experience in all His works, and that we should have knowledge in Nature's secrets, that nothing may be wanting, but that we should know it.

'In this wise were discovered many great arts such as would be tedious to relate.

'As it is God's will that we should know these things, He only can teach them to us, for such knowledge is not of man. Who can tell how letters were invented? Only by divine inspiration, for it pleased God that we should have such knowledge, therefore has man learned it.

'Even as God created His miraculous works, that man should know them, He also created a school wherein we learn this knowledge, but this school is not visible or known to everyone.

'The fisherman draws fish that he never saw from many fathoms beneath the water, the miner brings gold from the depths out of the earth, through which his sight cannot pierce. In this wise has God taught it.

'As there is nothing so occult that it shall not become manifest, so the same must be made known. Be it in the celestial firmament, in the sea, in the earth, all things must become manifest; but through man who discovers all things.

'Who will now show the first teacher and point with the finger at him? For he is not of Adam; but in him acts, and through him becomes manifested in his creatures all that is within him. He teaches it.

'To describe the courses this world will pass through in 24 years is lamentable enough. That man should have made himself so greedy and should have so wholly deluded himself and have failed to realise that his days must needs thereby be shortened; and that man should so wholly have forgotten God, his master, and should live not in accordance with His Law. To understand this requires the consideration of the mysteries shown by the signs of the Sun, the Moon and the Stars. It is also a subject for contemplation in what manner the people on earth inflict misery on each other, whereby no one will grant his fellow that the Sun shall shine upon him.

'There is but one number alone wherein we should walk upon earth, that is the One, and we should not count more. In God there are three, but the three are one.

'Thus we men, as God transmutes Himself into one, we likewise on earth should resign ourselves and become one.

'In that number and in no other is there rest and peace (Unity).

'That which is more than this is full of unrest and contention, one against the other.

'For if a reckoner puts a number and counts more than one, how many are the errors in root and result? Hence comes the dire distress and the worm gnawing us.

'How pleasant and good it is when we walk in the One! Heaven has also its physical course in that number; the earth and all are therein contained. 'But when that is not, then the Sun, Moon and Stars appear as signs that have to be considered.

'The end however is not yet, although there are signs thereof, but the calamity is only beginning.

'Blessed is he that sitteth not in the chair of pestilence, and who doth not dwell with sinners, for they shall be visited.

'Every man that is against God may know in his own conscience that he shall not prevail against nor overcome Him.

'It is hard to oppose Him, and no one is able to overcome Him. Therefore it is a great folly that man should strive against what is impossible to overcome.

'Thus there are 32 Symbols of that which is to be. May they not fly higher, so they but fall into the time for which they are intended.

'They are brought forth in all humility, but their course is through much misery. For as a serpent will they wind and turn until the end comes.

'But who would therefore grieve as the salvation from all arrogance and pride draweth nigh?

'Who would not rejoice that again the One shall be the Shepherd, and in the One shall be set the habitation? 'How peaceful will it be when there shall be no need for counting and numbers.

'Then will the precious ointment be poured upon the beard of Aaron, giving blessing from above. Then will the blessing issue from God.

'Even as there was no weeping in Heaven at the casting out of Lucifer into the abyss of Hell, why should it trouble us if in like manner Pride fall, so that One only and not more be in the Government?

'For many years past changes in the world have been foretold, but the signs indicated only the beginning. The end is not yet in operation, only the beginning.

'But the time of the nations is now at hand that they shall come to an end. And also that the just may not be seduced must the breaking-up take place.

'To me it is not known whom God will accept, but without regard to them all is the Prognostication set forth.

'Others may better discern this than I and understand whom it concerns.

'Thus hath the Kabbala given it, as a mother and beginner of Astronomy.

'The course of things is however so secret that they are right before us and yet we know of them only when they are already past.

'For everyone should know that it is not the Will of God they should not be converted and that they should not be saved from their doom.

'Therefore are the things seen with seeing eyes, and yet they are not seen.

'Let no one cast suspicion on anyone but let the End generate all things.

'Many speak and write, each one according to his ability. What others have also in this wise made, I will not reject, for the

forerunners are many when such Monarchy is to be dissolved.'
DIXI

The Magic Figures

The First Figure

'What a thing is internally is shown by its outward sign. As Nature signs her own so doth *Magic*. Thou has been signed as a devourer of all who have to do with thee. Blessed is he that is unsoiled of thee for thou leavest none in peace. *Magic* hath considered thee well and given thee thy due, but as thy beauty is only beheld and not the signs, therefore thou devourest all that touch thee. For beauty and not goodness is sought of thee.'

The Second Figure

'A flower groweth to the destined height. He that causeth her to grow also causeth her to fade. This happens to thee, for *Magic* hath therewith adorned thee, that thy coming up should be known, and also how thou has come to nought. For before thou wast, *Magic* hath known thee and therefore compared thee to a flower, that to-day is in bloom and to-morrow is withered. Wisdom and Fear of God would have preserved thee, but thou has overlooked it, thine own wisdom hath seduced thee.'

The Third Figure

'In good peace hast thou been sitting, but thou hast not known it, and hast allowed thyself to be moved. Thy wilfulness hath overturned and divided thee and no more shalt thou have thy former glory. Therefore art thou humbled and hast again become what thou wast formerly. Thou shouldst have been of aid and use to the whole world, and shouldst have set at rest others as well as thyself, but thou hast been seduced by what was rejected by thy forefathers. Although thou wilt repent, yet no one will rejoice through thee.'

The Fourth Figure

'Thou hast divided duty into left and right, as if it were oppressing thee. Both sides will cause thee anxiety and hatred shall altogether overcome thee. For a harlot divideth her wantonness and for a while she hath her way, but woe to her when her deceit is discovered. Then cometh true the saying, "no love without pain." Although thou didst mightily rejoice that thou art without a head, a head shall be placed upon thee and thou shall become a limb, though thou art not accustomed to it. But against thy will shalt thou swallow and eat what is not thy natural food.'

The Fifth Figure

'Thou hast not had the wisdom of thy crown, but has turned against the way of the crown, and hast done much evil. A stone shall fall upon thee that will press thee hard against thy will. For thou hast shed innocent blood and wast unwilling to know that which thou shouldst have known and what belongeth to a crown. He whom thou hast despised shall visit thee from the South and from the East, ere thou canst count two or three, and having recourse to thy allies will not avail thee for they themselves will fall.'

The Sixth Figure

'Thy flavour is strong, not wholesome and pleasant to everyone. Therefore, will thine enemies, to whom thou art not wholesome, cast a shadow and dry thee up, that thou mayest become temperate, and that thy fruit may not grow from thee as thou now vainly imaginest. For thou wilt have to give way to one whom thou knowest not. At the beginning thou wast very bold, and as a hero hast thou uplifted thyself. But thy undertaking hath divided thy comrades and what is divided hath no permanence. Still thou shalt retain a praise and a victory, for thou has known thyself.'

The Seventh Figure

'Because from time to time thou hast been self-willed thou art predestined to be surrounded by much adversity. For thou hast not considered of thyself how thou art prefigured magically under the symbol of a stone, as both fat and lean. Thou dost not know it, therefore thou fallest beneath the punishment that hath broken up all empires. Had thy pretended wisdom and understanding been thine own thou wouldst have been beyond disaster, and moreover other empires would have taken thee as a mirror. But it is not so, therefore thy wisdom proveth to be a folly at this time.'

The Eighth Figure

'Who is he that knoweth on whom the Sun shines, or to whom it shall give, what man by himself can in no wise take? Therefore because it is in the hand of God and He giveth it to whom He wills, thence follows it that man's resistance is in vain. For the hour hath come that thou shalt cease to be, notwithstanding thy strength, thy allies, thy power. For all thou hast established shall fall with thee, thou shalt delude thyself and others to thy own pity.'

The Ninth Figure

'Although God hath ordained that people should fear and be in terror of thee, yet there is a rod awaiting thee, that at the time shall smite thy back in such a wise as thou wilt not be able to endure, and they will say with amazement: Who would have thought that he would thus be brought to silence? It would have well become thee to observe moderation, and not as is now made manifest, to appear to be what thou art not, but to consider the end. This will make thee lame and crooked, that thou and thy followers shall with pain lament to each other.'

The Tenth Figure

'Thine is not a wedding garment, *Magic* has opened thy heart, and had made thee known. Therefore even as gold and silver must be refined from blemish, and tested, even seven times more severely than gold and silver is cleansed of its dross by fire, must thou be tried. It were well for thee to consider in thyself what was thy beginning, when thy neighbours brought thee up, and showed more kindness unto thee than was thy due, whereon thou hast presumed. This is demanded of thee. Thy transient wealth belongeth to another.'

The Eleventh Figure

'Although the sun did once shine upon thee, and thou hast glutted thyself with food and plunder, and wast sitting among the honeycombs, yet thou hast not wisely considered the end, and hast forgotten the winter; therefore he taketh away thy pleasure, and will compel thee to suck thine own paws. For as thou art bear-like, and has no further reason, Magic hath driven thee into the toils that thou shouldst be known. But if the wit of man had been thine, the winter would not have overtaken thee.'

The Twelfth Figure

'Although one may seat himself securely, yet there is no chair that may not fall, and also he that sitteth thereon. And thou seatest thyself upon this chair but thou shouldst not be thereon. Thou shouldst be below and not above. For thou art a burthen and an unbearable yoke, therefore falls *S. P.* Thou hast seated thyself thereon and he hath paid thee and given thee the reward thou was seeking: Temporal honour and praise: and these thou hast gathered all together in thyself and swallowed them up. Therefore as a temporal thing thou must also pass away.'

The Thirteenth Figure

'Too much kindness giveth too much evil, when the evil despiseth the kindness and the folly thereof allows it to advance in its undertaking. But it advanceth the wrong way, and it shall happen as to grass that is fully grown, it is mowed off and taken to where it should be. But if thou hadst been provident, and considered the end, thou wouldst see thy misery and know thyself. Nay, then, as thou willest it, shall it take its reward and its end, as thou hast been seeking it, and thy wisdom shall come to thee as a mockery.'

The Fourteenth Figure

'Giving too much out of hand bringeth sorrow and want to the giver; for if it fail he shall be beaten with his own weapons. Therefore as such overmuch giving away hath made thee proud, thy pride shall have a time and term where it goeth thus far and no farther; then shall all be torn up, and thou must, have nothing more. But if thou hadst considered that no one should set himself against the poor, and hadst also recognised thy liberty to be against thy neighbour, thou wouldst have abstained therefrom. But thy own heart hath seduced thee and thy wisdom hath been reckoned openly as a folly.'

The Fifteenth Figure

'Nothing is so good that it may not also become evil if it ever is without a head. To be without a head giveth pride and that bringeth forth no good. Therefore shall a head be placed upon thee that thou shalt become a limb, and it will press heavy upon thee, that thou shalt have to carry the head with the other limbs. It is high enough but it would be higher, didst thou but understand it. Thou shalt encounter those whom thou hast not expected, and thy great Council will cause confusion. But when thou sleepest will union take place.'

The Sixteenth Figure

'A child that goes to school and learns, when it arrives at years of discretion is ashamed of its childish work and destroys it. Thus shall it also happen to thee. As thou writest in such a manner thine own work shall be nought. For which reason there will be much labour for nought and in vain. For the time teacheth and giveth knowledge that not every pearl is a true pearl that is alleged so to be. Therefore a hand shall fall upon thee that will tear thee to shreds.'

The Seventeenth Figure

'He who buildeth a house should guard it, that when the enemy cometh it may not be destroyed. Its destruction should also be guarded that it may not be rebuilt, and that the folly of both may not be laughed at. Thus what hath been broken up is again rebuilt. Such things are done by children of men who do not consider the end. They erect, ornament and decorate, forgetting that their work is subject to destruction and again to restoration. At present all is still fragile, moreover they do not build on a rock but upon the sand.'

The Eighteenth Figure

'The eagle doth not grow out of thee, therefore shall He send a wind unto thee that will repress thee and thy young. Although it may go well with thee and thou sayest to thyself: My soul, thou hast all thou desirest and wishest for, what is there that may not be thine? Thou art sitting in Paradise. While thou art thinking it thus with thee, and there is nothing contrary, in thy greatest councils and rejoicings, the Deluge shall burst in upon thee, and the rough South Wind shall blow thee away as dust off the earth. For not in pleasure and wealth are we created but in the vale of tears. This thou hast forgotten.'

50

The Nineteenth Figure

'Thou art leaping about in thy garden and art well pleased with thyself; but giving up thy wisdom and following thy pleasure thou makest bad use of thy leapings. Therefore shall it happen to thee even as thou art lying there, and those that should be thy peace will hunt thee and force thee to leap high. But take thought with thyself and consider that human things are vain. Then wouldst thou become altogether changed and wouldest be safe from the misfortune into which thou doest daily walk. Bethink thyself that pride and ill-manners never ended well.

The Twentieth Figure

'A thing standeth upright as long as it can be upheld; but when man alone uplifteth, then in its time, the highest will become lowest. In this wise shall man set his wisdom against the earth and bury it therein, from whence it hath come, and it shall give way to another. For human wisdom may last for a time. She is compared to a flower in the field, that is lovely and pleasing in herself. But the flower doth not remain, much less human wisdom. It is said "Time bringeth roses," but these also fade. Thus shall it happen to thee, because thou art of thyself.'

The Twenty-First Figure

'When rest shall come to him, and thy watchers shall be dispersed, and thy limehound shall be wearied and succumb, then shalt thou be afflicted in thine own nest, with thy young, and shalt be forced to give way to him of whom thou hadst supposed that he would give way to thee, and thou shalt have to leave thy eggs and nest. Thus shall happen to thee, that thou and thine shall be ensnared together in the meshes thou has laid for others, and never again shalt thou be what thou wast formerly. And the children that were thine shall no more be thine. Thy robe shall clothe thine enemy, who will despise thee.'

The Twenty-Second Figure

'Although thou hast not wholly revealed thy heart, yet there is nothing that in its time will remain secret and not be revealed. Then shalt thou become known to him that should know thee. For thou didst and wouldst presume to subjugate the soft in silken and the hard in iron clothing, and wast thinking in thy councils: Now may we not what we would, who are they that shall prevent us? Nay, truly, it will be the soft at first, the iron afterward, but it will cost thine own blood. Didst thou but think of humility, not of the kingdom of this world, how well would it be with thee.'

The Twenty-Third Figure

'As there are three persons in the Godhead, comprising but one number, thus should also men become united only in one number. But, where this does not come to pass then is fulfilled the saying: every empire that is divided in itself must pass away. Thus no empire passeth away unless it be divided against itself. The wisest construction of a house and confederation of an empire is, when they conduct themselves as one and act accordingly, so that the number may never be divided. For what can be divided is unstable and vain, and one disputes with another. But rejoice, for thou shalt become one.'

The Twenty-Fourth Figure

'What is it, or what does it help you that ye combine together and do not consider that ye are contrary in soul and heart? Behold only how ye are externally marked by your garments, even so are ye also internally. Ye should not be as beasts but as men, but as ye are not so, he will rule you that is above you, of whom stands written: give unto him what to him belongs. For no bestial reason is permanent, only that reason remaineth which is destined and ordained by God. This falleth in due time, thus is your council destroyed.'

The Twenty-Fifth Figure

'A thing must be understood as certain and true in order to be known without any doubt. But for this reason, that finite knowledge had faults and defects in thy design, therefore has thou been strangled in thine own doubts. Thou hast supposed that there is no need for closing with the true seal, and hast thought to be a seal thyself; but therein thou wast in error and art not what thou hast supposed thyself to be. This will give thee a miserable death. For thou hast lived on and on in doubt, and others with thee have built upon sand. They have wept, and thou shalt weep yet more.'

The Twenty-Sixth Figure

'The Sybil hath been mindful of thee when she placed the "F," and right well art thou now standing in the rose; for thou art ripe and time hath brought thee. What the Sybil saith of thee shall be accomplished and even more shall be said of thee. The summer that bringeth roses is that contrary time wherein all things are divided; which is an indication that man was building on sand. This must pass away, and thou shalt set it upon the rock that many will be astounded. For when the time cometh, also therewith cometh that wherefore the time hath come.'

The Twenty-Seventh Figure

'It hath been forgotten that many heads rule badly, and that also only one should rule and not more. This is the cause that they have split up and parted, each one seeking his own opportunity. But as it is not right to seek one's own opportunity, but that each should serve the other, and seek to be useful to the other, and leave his own, as doth indeed but seldom happen, for this reason they will be put down; and to whom it is destined to be united, he shall be foremost, and under him shall rejoice those who have been long afflicted and distressed.'

The Twenty-Eighth Figure

'There will be no common voice, therefore it will be in vain that the five consult together. Have care of the future-forty-two and a little before and after will he come and do as he pleaseth, and bend you like a branch, and gird you in a wise such as will not please you. For thy council is not of him who is sought nor of whom thou deemest it to be. If ye would consider that there is no wisdom at all in man when he throweth off the yoke, he would himself be opposed to it and would not throw off the yoke, but would think of the heavy reckoning in the day of wrath.'

The Twenty-Ninth Figure

'Thus shall it come to pass that each one will be led into its own pasture. For feeding in strange pasture causeth distress, contention, and misery in this world. As soon as each one cometh into its own stall there shall be unity. For the mouth becometh depraved, feeding according to its lust as it pleaseth the jaws; all that cometh of going into strange pastures. How blessed shall be the hour, and the poverty, that will come and shall ordain each one to its meadow, not far from the year XXXXIII.'

The Thirtieth Figure

'Thou hast often assembled, and much congregated, but the enemy was not with thee, therefore all things thou hast resolved were to no purpose and in vain. It must be alone that thou wilt forgo thy claims, and reflect of whom thou art, of whom thou hast learnt, and what thou wouldst do if thou wert to turn aside, and wouldst acknowledge thyself and others; then wouldst thou cease. But as thou desirest to be what thou shouldst not be, and wilt sit upon the chair of Saint Peter, and whereas the same must fall; therefore thou mayest not continue in thy plots, for he shall turn aside thy design who is thy master.'

The Thirty-First Figure

'There shall be such a total renewal and change that they will be as children that know nothing of the cunning and intrigues of the old. This shall be when they count LX, a little less, but not more.[2] Therefore it is well that we should remember that the time appeareth to be a long time according to a man's lifetime, but as a short time should we observe and consider it. For to cause so much to fall and to be overthrown, with such a raging and roaring lion that has so long grown, this cannot be done in a moment. But how well shall it be with him that shall be as a little child, for human knowledge causeth but unrest and grief.'

The Thirty-Second Figure

'Thou hast taken great trouble, therefore it is but just that after thy day's work thou shouldst have rest and repose. Blessed is he that is born during sleep; he shall know no evil. For thou hast purified with great care, and hast endured much in thy days, Thee no one hath overcome, and no one shall there be that will again awaken thee, even as long as there is counted as much as thine enemies have counted from their eyrie.'

Elucidations Of The Prognostications And Conclusion Of Doctor Paracelsus

THESE Elucidations of the Prognostications and Conclusion of Doctor Paracelsus are given in the Strassburg edition of his works:

'The symbolical figures as above stated are 32 and will take their complete course in 42 (? 420) years.

'It is not less; the least of them (I) would require a larger book to describe than the one wherein they are all comprised.

'If all these symbolical figures were to be adequately described, with complete explanation, how much distress would there be found in them? Reedlike inconstancy, and the multitude of its associations will run into each other in such strange confusion and will happen in such an unexpected way as is hardly to be credited.

'For many things are written in an occult sense which it is not well to relate.

'Thus is the Symbol (II) compared to a Lily[3]; but it should not be lilies but Toads. For a toad is the first given Magic Sign. But it is changed from a toad into a flower. For even as a toad inflates itself with poison, likewise does he inflate himself who is given to pride. It is not a garden lily but a lily growing out of thorns, that refuses to grant her fragrance to anyone.

III. 'There will be distress and violence suffered. What follows, were it understood and believed, would never give rise to much laughter. For to be forsaken by the best companions makes a man weak and dull. And furthermore if he is to be attacked that was so well cared for, and who is the child of the house, it is well to remember that there is need of time, strength, cunning and watchfulness.

'It would be well could the time be spared to describe it, not only in general terms but in particular detail; then would much distress become revealed.

IV to VIII. 'The other four symbols follow after the first mentioned, and will also demolish much, until each one in turn is fulfilled.

'They will seek much assistance from strangers, and bind one chain into another, and will erect and again let fall, break and make, and seek hither and thither where shelter from the heat may be found.

'But the eighth symbol shall gain the victory and triumph.

'For if that were not to come to pass it would be impossible that on earth there should ever again be rest or peace so long as the world endures.

'So totally will everyone act according to his will and forget why the are on earth, but only declare: thus I will, thus I do.

IX. 'Although there is need to bend a rod firmly, otherwise it returns again to the straight line, it should be borne in mind that nothing crooked can so remain, but must be allowed to return again to its straightness.

'Were this not to happen, very slowly wouldst thou be unbent, so that thou wouldst not be able to come to the length wherewith thou wouldst fain be contented.

X. 'The following symbol would do wisely to withdraw into itself, and contemplate itself, surrendering its own will, and seat itself in ashes and sackcloth.

'For what is this but Nineveh? Would to God that by prayer the prophecy may be averted, as was the prophecy of Jonah.

XI. 'To munch the paws is a meagre diet, and it is painful to freeze after sunshine.

'But what one does of one's own choice, one must one's self have.

XII. 'It is a great thing that the Virgin Mary has spoken, that He has deposed the mighty ones from the chair. Therefore let no one marvel that impossible things come to pass, for these are in the hand of God.

XIII. 'Therefore let him that is very proud humble himself, for the hungry are fed, and that which should not be is cut down.

XIV. 'Happy are the poor, they are not forsaken, and he who has no other aid than the Letter, and is bound to the Letter, how can he prevent that a hole be pierced therein?

XV. 'In the course of time it has gone on and on and it has seemed to reach well nigh the height of the Tower of Babel.

'Even as this Tower was forsaken miraculously amidst confusion of tongues, in the same wise a roof falls from above and higher than this it is impossible to build.

XVI. 'And although much is written, yet no one can triumph against the same.

XVII. 'Therefore must thou perforce be pleased to replace the stone from whence thou hast taken it.

XVIII. 'And thou must allow the winds to buffet thee about, for thou hast not built a wall against them.

XIX. 'And thy leap shall displease thee alone, and not many more.

XX. 'Who may know but only the wise man what aim is set, and how man of himself sets up what should not be?

'Since all things stand in God's hand, how can man use his strength, which is nought but a reed?

XXI. 'Hence cometh failure. Then shall he be subdued who has secretly kept many in his pay, but before this befalls the next symbol will be fulfilled.

XIII. 'For if one does not cleanse his own house how shall he cleanse that of another?

'If a man does not wisely manage that which is his own, much less can he manage that which is another's.

XXIII. 'Then the rivals shall cease to contend, for all things shall be settled in peace and concord.

XXIV. 'Therefore also alliances must be dissolved that were only made to cause discord and to accomplish the heart's desire.

XXV. 'Although God has for a long time looked on to see what man would do, and how he would apply his wisdom, yet is it directed to nothing permanent nor certain, albeit he so persuades himself. This must cease.

XXVIII and XXX. 'Doubt not, for doubt is the foe of Faith. It must be firm as a rock and enlightened, as it was in the beginning, otherwise it is not enduring and is hurtful withal.

XXVI. 'For the Sun shall enlighten him that will be judge of himself.

XXVII and XXIX. 'And neither alliances nor chains shall there be strong enough to hinder each from being harnessed to his own plough, even as is ordained for him.

XXXI. 'And as children without cunning or guile shall they appear.

XXXII. 'This one has often brought about peace, and has thereafter brought peace to himself. But he has many times been again awakened. When he rouses himself all creatures tremble before him.

'He is that that reverses and judges as seems good to him, and he has determined to act yet 24 years until again he rests.

'To him such time is but a moment. To us he leaves the tedious length thereof.

'He does not indeed each year do away with one symbol, but simultaneously fulfils them all and altogether as one, until all is completed and accomplished.

'Who may understand who it is that is hereby intended?

'Hence may none be named, and none be suspected, until all has come to pass. For thus it shall be.

'Whoever therefore may read this Prediction should read it bearing in mind that he inform no one. For no one is in the knowledge.

'But when a thing has been accomplished and has come to pass, everyone can afterwards understand it, but it is then no more of use.

'Many a one will think to himself that it does not concern him, and yet perchance it may do so.

'For it is usual for everyone to. wish to protect himself but no one is willing to know himself.

'They ever place the interpretation as having allusion to those against whom they feel envy, opposing God even, and he who judges shall perhaps himself be judged, and he who deems himself to be perfect and whole, may possibly be ragged and torn at the sides.

'May God give a good End.'

Another Prognostication By Theophrastus Paracelsus

'I BEAR in mind that you may not believe me when I tell you that my (at this time) despised writings shall yet be held in great value and esteem by wise and judicious men.

'It will, however, not happen until the great and fearful eclipse of the sun is past.

'I say that then there shall overflow as the waters of a mighty river all kinds of revolts, riots, wars, slaughter, murders, conflagrations and all evil into the northern countries.

'Then beware Brabant, Flanders and Zealand, and ye who like my Swiss countrymen feed upon cheese.

'Then will the Lily be altogether decayed, exhausted and cast down.

'In the same wise will the Eagle be plucked, dishonoured, insulted and despised.

'Othman will be foremost and the Eagle shall cringe before him.

'Good times shall then be. Fruit and what is necessary for life will thrive, but the poor will enjoy little thereof.

'The Spiritual will grow and increase as the Moon.

'Then those of the East will for a time have a great Victory and exalt the Golden Tower.

'The people without a head will not remain untouched.

'Then shall the high nobility be punished as though they were criminals.

'The Lion having Blue and White for associates will march in, in a high manner.

'Beware, thou beautiful City, that wast formerly a lustre and eye of Europe.

'The Rue-wreath dwindles to nought. Doth there not remain of this conflagration one spark, that shall soon after begin to burn and light an inextinguishable fire?

'Now when these things come to pass, neither truth, nor faith, nor fidelity, nor honour will be esteemed.

'But there will be many truths, many fidelities, many honours; but they will be of such a kind that they may be known and considered as no faith, no truth, no fidelity and no honour.

'The White will for some time overcome the Black with the Black and will accomplish great things.

'The Pomegranate will burst and throw out his seeds and will let them perish.

'Then shall the Rue-plant or Rue-wreath incline its root or natural origin to the Lily and shall stand as a shield before her, that the Wind of Health may not blow upon her.

'The people of the earth shall then be in commotion, and no ties of brotherhood, marriage or friendship will be respected.

'The Lion will join himself to the Fishes.

'And the Crown will be subject to the Fine Hat.

'Then will the Rue-wreath be soiled with Milk.

'And the Pelican shall be devoured by his young.

'But the Phoenix shall be consumed in the fire, and when the dew moistens the ashes he will again revive according to his Nature.

'But he will become a noble Phoenix, and will press hard upon the Toad, and he will take to the Lion and will give him a choice.

'The Lion will select the best and no more.

'Upon the other Wild Horse this Phoenix will place a bridle and will ride it with spurs but without a saddle.

'Then a new generation of beasts with various strange heads shall be born. They will have many mouths and stomachs, but only one natural draught.

'The most profligate will maintain his magnificence, and his angels will be clothed in blood. They will be intent upon one work alone.

'A pair of horses will appear and in all places will the wail of the fugitives be heard.

'The Dragon of Sleep will cause the Eagle to become weary of all magnificence.

'The Fountain of Life will commence to flow.

'And a white Eagle will be changed into black.

'Milk and Blood will decrease, and the animal Tree will begin to grow.

'An old Lion will be bound and a young Lion will become free. He will please all those animals which the old had vexed.

'He will do even more, for he will change his mane and hair into silk.

'The Bear will lay snares, and the Ox-head will seek to gore him.

'The Griffin will fly over him but will not harm him.

'Then shall the Pearl, so long lost, be found by one of humble estate, and will be set, as a jewel, in gold.

'It will be given to the Prince of all beasts, that is, to the right Lion.

'He will hang it about his neck, and wear it with honour.

'He will resist the Bear and the Wolf, and rend them asunder; so that the beasts of the forest shall be safe.

'Then will the Old Art flourish and no heed will be given to the New.

'Then will the New World begin, and the White and the Black shall disappear.

'All Vain glory will be ended, and the plumes of the bird of the East shall be burnt by the Sun of the South.

'How then will it be with thee, Oh thou Lion and earthly one who art painted and bound with gold?

'All thy doings shall be changed, and the seven heads shall become one head.

'Out of this one, a head shall be born that shall be armed with a horn.

'This horn shall bruise all that which has so long brought sorrow to Iffinos.

'And the great City shall be the head of the less and shall become free from servitude.

'Europe shall be the head, Asia the crown, but Africa shall be the jewel.

Epilogue

THESE are the famous Prophecies of Theophrastus Paracelsus, considered by Eliphas Lévi to be 'the most astounding monument and indisputable proof of the reality and existence of the gift of natural prophecy.'

The Prophecies or Prognostications do not merely relate to events that happened in the age of the Reformation, and do not refer strictly to 24 or 42 years after they were published, but suggest events that happened long after, some that are even now happening, and others that will happen in the future.

Nearly four centuries have elapsed since these predictions were made. I have neither altered nor suppressed any of them, but only translated from the old German to the best of my ability.

Whatever interpretation may be given to these predictions their ancient origin cannot be disputed.

They were first published about the year 1530, and are extant in print of that period. It is true the first editions give no date, and it is uncertain whether the Latin edition preceded the German, as the latter shows more originality of expression. It is by no means improbable that the Latin version referred to by Eliphas Lévi may be only a translation.

The German edition Of 1530, which is also found reprinted in the works of Paracelsus collected by Johann Huser and published at Strassburg in the year 1616, was taken as the original for the present translation. The Prophecies occur in vol. ii, pp. 594-608.

The Plates have also been reproduced from the old woodcuts of that edition.

The original Manuscript of Paracelsus is said to be in the Court
Library of the
Grand Duke of Baden at Karlsruhe.

Interpretation

To interpret a prophecy is more hazardous than to make one, for a prophecy may be vague, but an interpretation is expected to be exact.

I will not venture to interpret any of the predictions, but only chance to suggest the meaning of some of them.

Ingenious readers are welcome to interpret each and all of the Prophecies in their own way. It may interest those fond of historical research or who are keenly following the course of political events.

Religion also plays a large part in the predictions.

As history repeats itself, a prediction thought to have been accomplished by a country, person or event,, may again be verified by another or similar occurrence.

Paracelsus apparently saw the future as a series of cinematograph pictures before him, but describes without chronological sequence.

As a whole the figures and chapters relate either to the Church or to the State.

Thus IV, VII, X, XII, XV, XX, XXII, XXIII, XXV, XXVIII to XXXII apparently refer to religious or ecclesiastical affairs, while the rest of the figures and prognostications relate to social and political changes.

Figures and Chapters I, II are evidently intended for France.

VI is a striking prediction of Napoleon on St. Helena. The laurel branch on a rock.

III, V, VIII may fit Kaiser Wilhelm.

IX, 'The wild Lion, that is Bohemia, will again enter the Church,' etc. Paracelsus Opera, Strassburg ed., vol. ii, p. 625.

IV, VII, X, XII, XV, XXVIII, XXX relate to the Pope and the Catholic Church.

XVI, Old Theology.

XVII, XXIX, XXXI, The New Religion.

XVIII, XIX, Germany.

XIII, XIV, Austria.

XX, Materialism.

XXI, The Turk drowning in the Bosphorus, and of Turkey in Europe.

XXII, Knight and Monk, Aristocracy and Clergy.

XXIII, While Theology disputes, the Mystic steals away the Truth of Religion.

XXIV, A strange forecast.

XXV, Rationalism.

XXVI, The mysterious Prophecy.

XXVII, The Balkan federation?

XXXII, The Guide of the World.

Notes

[←1] Quoted in Stoddart's *Life of Paracelsus*.

[←2]   When LVX, Lux, Light, comes.

[←3]

Franciscum, 1658.--J. K.

The Royal Symbol of France was in ancient times three Toads. It is not certain when

Lilies were first adopted instead, but Charles VI introduced the three Lilies that have

since then been identified with the French Royal Coat of Arms. *See* I. Chifflé, *Lilium*

Table des matières